Canadian Picture Dictionary

100

MELODY VILLAGE JUNIOR SCHOOL
TORONTO DISTRICT SCHOOL BOARD
520 SILVERSTONE DRIVE
TORONTO, ON   M9V 3L5

D1318142

Illustrations by Maggie Swanson

Houghton Mifflin Canada Limited

Toronto   Boston   London   Sydney

MELODY VILLAGE JUNIOR SCHOOL
TORONTO DISTRICT SCHOOL BOARD
520 SILVERSTONE DRIVE
TORONTO, ON   M9V 3L5

Cover illustrations,
clockwise from top left:
turn, hundred, moon, apple.

Copyright © 1991 by Houghton Mifflin Canada Limited.
Copyright © 1986, 1989 by Houghton Mifflin Company. All
rights reserved. No part of this work may be reproduced or
transmitted in any form or by any means, electronic or
mechanical, including photocopying and recording, or
by any information storage or retrieval system without the
prior written permission of Houghton Mifflin Canada Limited,
unless such copying is expressly permitted by federal
copyright law.

Cover design   Ivan Holmes

Canadian Cataloguing in Publication Data
Main entry under title:

Canadian picture dictionary

ISBN 0-395-55005-X

1. Picture dictionaries, English — Juvenile literature.
I. Swanson, Maggie.

PE1629.C35 1990   j423'.1   C90-093420-4

Printed in Canada

5 6 7 8 9 11 04

Preface

HOUGHTON MIFFLIN CANADIAN PICTURE DICTIONARY
A Note to Teachers and Parents

A dictionary is a basic tool for reading and writing that everyone should learn to use. The *Houghton Mifflin Canadian Picture Dictionary* is specifically designed to provide the help and encouragement children in the preschool and early primary years need, and to prepare them for more advanced levels of dictionary use.

Fulfilling Children's Needs

During the preschool and early school years, children use a picture dictionary differently than they will later. Initially, they use it as a picture book: as a source of sheer enjoyment. Children also use it as a stimulus for expanded thinking by extending the associations they are beginning to make between words and objects, actions, or feelings. As children learn to read and write, a picture dictionary becomes a treasury of ideas, a source of words they may want to write, and an aid for reading unfamiliar words.

The *Houghton Mifflin Canadian Picture Dictionary* has been published to meet these needs. The openness of its design and the quality of its illustrators — all by Maggie Swanson, a distinguished children's illustrator — invite children to enter the book. Because children already "know" most words they will want to look up, words in this dictionary have been carefully chosen from studies of children's reading, speaking, and writing vocabularies. Some common words are not included in this dictionary because they cannot be illustrated effectively in pictures or with simple sentences that accurately show their meaning, and we want the *Houghton Mifflin Canadian Picture Dictionary* to provide information that children can readily understand. For example, children soon come to know a word like *fine*, meaning "excellent" or "in good health", from conversation, but it is difficult for a dictionary to convey this meaning, and lacking meaning, children will be frustrated in finding its spelling. Even so, this dictionary contains many high-frequency words, like *was* or *the* that are difficult for children to remember in reading or spelling. These words appear in context, highlighted in example sentences.

A special feature of this dictionary is found on nine full- or double-page illustrations at the back of the book that show how words relate to one another. A coloured border around an entry word in the dictionary itself means that word, together with related words, can be found on the pages with the same colour edges at the back of the book. Words in these pages are presented in attractive and familiar settings and are easy to see and read.

Another feature of this dictionary is the use of a number of family groupings whose members appear in illustrations and example sentences throughout the book. With continuing use of the *Picture Dictionary*, children will come to recognize these people and their pets as familiar friends.

Using this Dictionary

A picture dictionary should entertain, but this dictionary is designed to do much more. First, it can show a child what a "word" is. Second, by listing words in alphabetical order, it gives a child experience with the alphabet.

Third, this dictionary will help a child use aids such as words and pictures ("magic pictures") to find his or her place in a dictionary. When children are trying to find a word, these pictures help them to remember the sounds associated with initial letters.

Fourth, this dictionary will acquaint a child with simple cross references by using entry words with coloured borders, that refer to pages at the end of the book. Fifth, it can suggest interrelationships among words through the use of those pages, and develop other thinking skills. Sixth, its example sentences can serve as story starters.

Helping Children Get Started

To help a child get the most out of this dictionary, you may want to "walk through" *How to Use Your Picture Dictionary*. The section entitled "Look It Over" gives an overview of the dictionary. "How to Find a Word . . ." provides a step-by-step acquaintance with the many facets of the *Houghton Mifflin Canadian Picture Dictionary*.

Of course, you may want to provide the initial introduction yourself and save the more formal printed explanation until another time. Begin with an overview of the book, so children can get an idea of what's in it. Point out that many dictionary words are printed in special type in sentences that help children figure out what those words mean. Show some of the full- and double-page illustrations found at the end of the dictionary and talk about them. Allow the child opportunity to browse and ask questions.

At another time, tell children about the alphabetical sequence. Show them that all the words beginning with "a" are under the key picture "a," and so on.

Later, go through other letters of the alphabet in the same way. Eventually, pick out a word (like *game*) that is cross referenced to the illustrations at the back of the book and explain the cross-referencing system. Demonstrate and encourage the use of the dictionary as a source of ideas for writing and an aid to spelling.

The role of the teacher or parent should be that of initiator and interested associate. Help your children have fun with language, and success will surely follow.

How to Use Your

LOOK IT OVER

Your has a lot of words.

It can help you write words.
It can show you what words mean.
It can give you ideas for stories, too.

LOOK AT THE PAGES IN YOUR

The words are in A-B-C order.
Each word has a picture to show what it means.

FIND THE PAGES AT THE BACK OF YOUR

They have a coloured bar around them.
They have a lot more words and pictures.

HOW TO FIND A WORD IN YOUR

Words are in A-B-C order:

ABCDEFGHIJKLMNOPQRSTUVWXYZ

abcdefghijklmnopqrstuvwxyz

FIND **K**. See **K k** . Words that begin with the same sound as kite will begin with the letter **k**. The picture of kite will help you remember the first letter for kite.

Find **m**. Why is there a picture of ? Yes, monster begins with the sound for **m**. Monster will help you remember the sound for **m**.

DO YOU KNOW HOW TO SPELL A WORD? Then you can find it in the A-B-C order.

FIND many. Does many mean more than one?

FIND dream. Can you dream?

DO YOU KNOW JUST THE FIRST LETTER OF A WORD? Then you can find the word to see how to write it.

FIND . How do you spell the name?

DO YOU WANT TO WRITE ABOUT DINOSAURS?

FIND dinosaur. There is no picture! The ▬▬▬ tells you to go to the back of the book. Find the page with a ▬▬▬ What do you see? Now you can write about a lot of dinosaurs.

LOOK AT MORE PAGES WITH A COLOURED BAR. There are many things you can write about.

Now, have fun with your .

Aa

apple

a • an

A bear is in my room. Why is an old bear there?

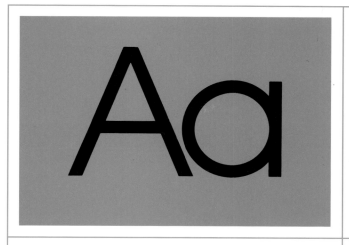

add

afraid

Max is afraid of the dog.

able

Max is able to climb.

afternoon

Dan takes a nap in the afternoon.

again

Jill slides. Now she slides again.

air

airplane

airport

all

We are all in the picture.

alphabet

The alphabet starts with **ABC**.

am

I am a boy!

angry

Freddie takes mother's steak. Mother is angry.

and   A bear and an owl are in my room.

animal

horse

elephant

wolf

answer

Dan can answer the telephone.

apple

answer

We add 2 and 2. The answer is 4.

are

We are girls!

ask

May Ling asks for a pencil.

asleep

The baby is asleep.

ate

Freddie ate all his food.

aunt

Aunt Pat is mother's sister.

boot

baby

babies

back

Dan has a number on his back.

bad

Freddie is a bad dog.

bag

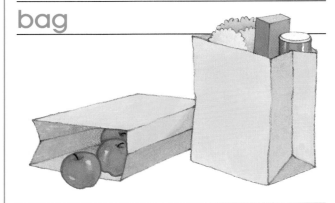

ball

balloon

banana

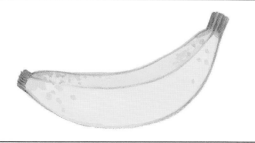

bark

The puppy barks at the cat.

barn

baseball

basket

basketball

bat

I hit the baseball with a bat.

bat

A bat is an animal. It can fly.

bath

We give Freddie a bath. We get wet.

bear

brown bear

panda

polar bear

teddy bear

beat

Can a turtle beat a rabbit in a race? Can the turtle win?

bed

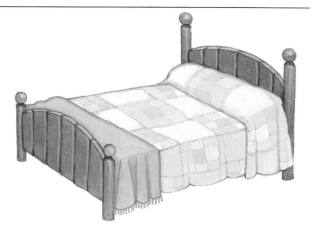

bell

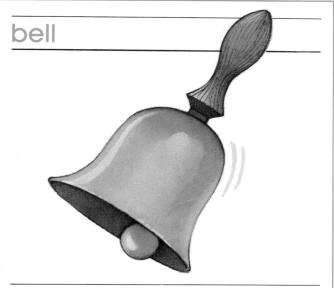

big

Freddie is big. His house is small.

bike

bird

cardinal

wren

blue jay

bite

Freddie takes a bite of Ching Wah's sandwich.

black

blow

María can blow up a balloon.

birthday

On my birthday I am six years old.

blue

board

Grandfather holds a big board.

boat

sailboat

motorboat

ferryboat

book

bowl

box

shoe box

boxes

cardboard box

toy box

boy

A boy is a young man.

branch

branches

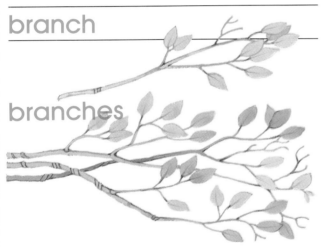

breath

Ramón can see his breath on the window.

bridge

break

Max breaks the cup.

brother

Rob is my brother. We have the same mother and father.

brown

bunch

Here is a bunch of flowers.

bunches

building

house   apartment building house   school

bunny

bunnies

burn

The wood burns.

bus

buses

button

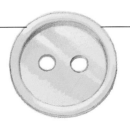

Ben can button his coat.

14

Cc

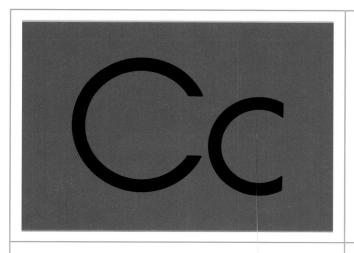

cat

cake

calendar

call

Ben can call grandmother.

camera

camp

can

Here is a can.

candy

candies

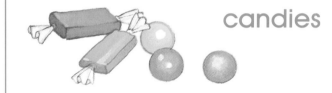

can

Aunt Pat says, "Yes, you can walk."

cannot

Aunt Pat says, "No, you cannot walk."

cap

car

card

carrot

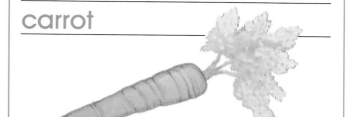

cartoon

A cartoon tells a story with pictures.

cat

catch

Freddie likes to catch the ball.

catcher

chicken

chief

Mr. Deer Fox is a chief.

CHIEF DEER FOX

chair

straight-back chair

rocking chair

armchair

child

A child is a young person.

children

church

churches

circle

circus • circuses

city • cities

classroom

clean

Freddie had a bath, and now Freddie is clean.

climb

Aunt Pat can climb the ladder.

clock

digital

cuckoo

desk

alarm

clothes

A shirt and coat are clothes.

coat

club

The children have a club. They plant trees together.

cold

Ice is cold. Jill is cold.

brrrr!

colour

See the colours.

colour

We colour the pictures.

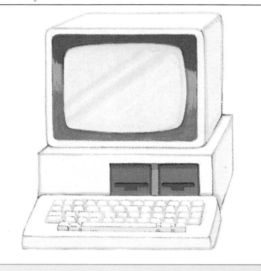

computer

cone

cook

Dad likes to cook.

cookie

cool

Jill blows on her apple to make it cool.

corn

count

Count the cubes. How many are there?

country

Our house is in the country.

cover

Jill takes the cover off the jar.

cow

cream

Father puts cream on his bananas.

cry

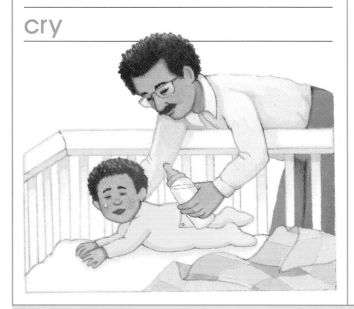

cube

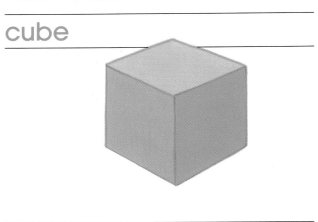

cup

mug

tea cup

mug

cut

Dd

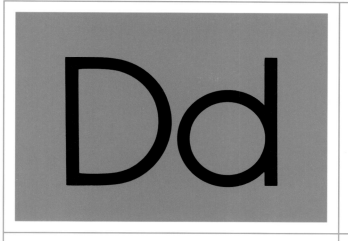

duck

dad • daddy

Fran calls her father dad.
Dan and Ben call their
father daddy.

daisy • daisies

dance

dark

It is dark, and Jill cannot
see.

day   Morning, afternoon, and night make one day.

dear

Annie starts a letter with "Dear Jack."

desk

dictionary

deer

Five deer are here.

dictionaries

did

Did Ben eat an orange?

dig

different

Alex and Buster are the same. Freddie is different.

dinner

dinosaur

do

How many pencils do you have?

doctor

does

Does Jill have four pencils?

dog

collie

mixed breed

beagle

terrier

doll

baby

rag

china

draw

dream

Annie has a dream.

dollar

door

cupboard door

entrance door

screen door

29

dress

dresses

dress

In the morning, we dress.

drink

Max can drink milk. Amy can drink milk too.

drive

drop

Here is a drop of water.

drop

Watch Fran drop her books.

drum

Ben has a drum.

dry

They dry Freddie.

duck

E e

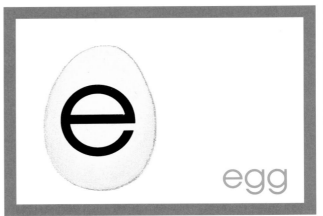

egg

ear

elephant

child

rabbit

earth

Here is the earth.

earth

Plants grow in the earth.

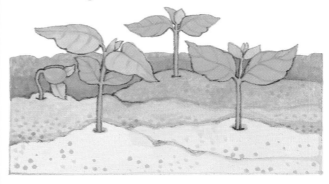

east

The sun rises in the east.

easy

Is it easy to ride a bike? It is easy for May Ling.

eat

Watch Freddie eat our dinner.

egg

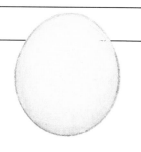

eight

end

equal

Two and two equals four.

evening

The sun sets in the evening.

everybody

Everybody laughs.

eyes

Ff

feather

face

Sara has paint on her face.

fairy • fairies

fall

See Humpty Dumpty fall off the wall.

fall

family

families

farm

fast

The train goes fast.

fat

Here is a fat cat.

father

I call my father dad.

feed

Watch Rob feed the duck.

fence

chain link

picket

field

finger

fight

fire

first   Fran is first in line.

first grade

fish • fishes

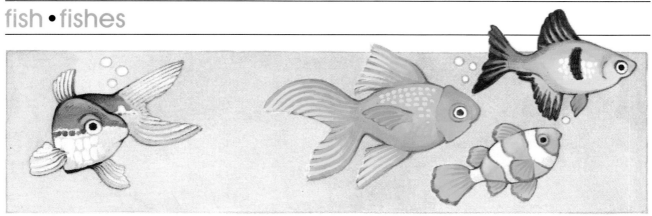

five

flat

floor

flower

The flower is red.

fly • flies

Flies are in the air.

fly

A plane can fly.

fly

May Ling hits a fly

food

foot

feet

football

forest

forget

Did Ben forget his **ABC's**?

A...B...C...

four

friend

fox

foxes

frog

funny

free

María gets a free kitten.

41

Gg

g ghost

game

garden

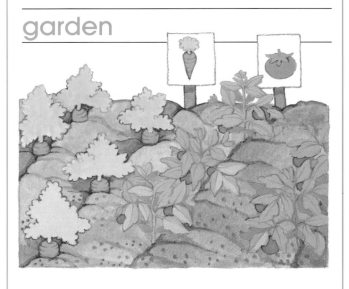

ghost

get

I get a book.

giant

girl

A girl is a young woman.

give

Give Ben a book.

glass

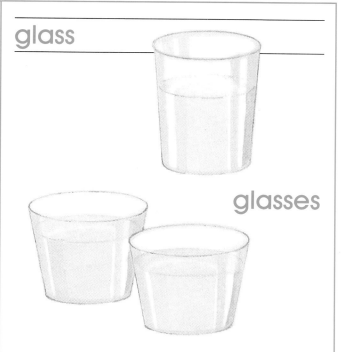

glasses

glasses

glue

go   The cars go.

goes   One car goes.

gold

goose

geese

grandfather

We call our grandfather grandpa.

grandmother

We call our grandmother grandma.

grass

green

grow

We see Fran grow.

guess

Hh

hat

had

Dan had an apple and a pear.

half

Here is half for you. Here is half for me.

hair

Halloween

hand

hard

It is hard to ride a bike up the hill.

hang

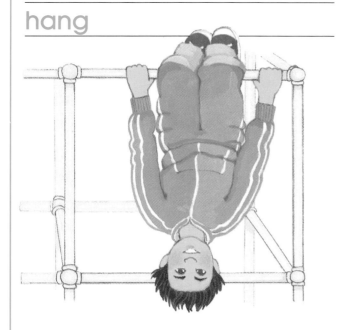

happy

hard

The walk is hard.

has

Dan has an apple and a pear.

hat

police

top

firefighter

baseball

have

Dan and Ben have apples and pears.

head

One turtle has his head out. One turtle has his head in.

he

He is Sam.

heart

her

Her sweater is blue.

here

Write your name here.

high

The balloon is high in the sky.

hill

hide

his

His sweater is green.

hit

Ben can hit the ball.

hold

María holds the cup.

hole

home

Home is the place where we live.

horse

hospital

hot

The sun is hot. Jill is hot.

hour

An hour is part of a day.

house

how many

How many raccoons do you see? I see six!

hundred

100

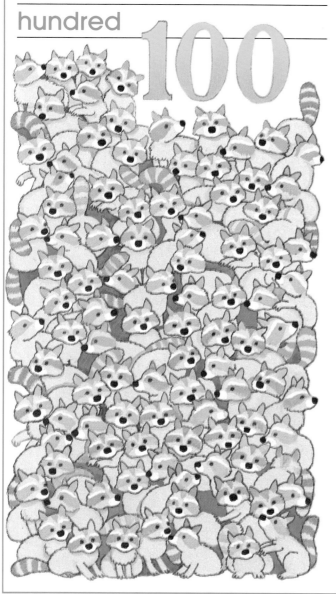

hungry

Freddie is hungry.

hunt

Father hunts for his keys.

hurt

Max hurt his leg.

Ii

igloo

I

I am Dan.

ice

I skate on the ice.

is

He is Rob. She is Fran.

it

It is a kitten.

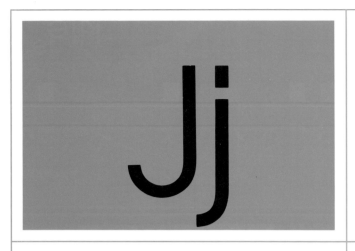

Jj

jack-in-the-box

jar

Here is the jar.

jet

juice

The juice is in a glass.

jump

Ben can jump.

54

Kk

kite

kick

king

kindergarten

kiss • kisses

María gives mother a kiss.

kitchen

kite

The kite goes high.

kitten

knock

Watch Ben knock.

lamp

ladder

lake

A lake is bigger than a pond.

lady • ladies

land

The people see land.

land

Watch the plane land.

large

Large is big.

laugh

leaf

leaves

leave

Watch grandmother leave.
She goes in a car.

left

Here is Ben's left hand.

leg

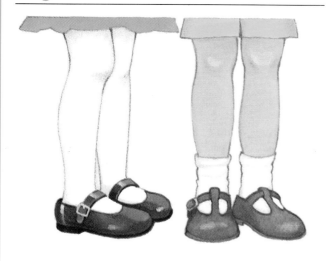

letter

The first letter is **A.**

letter

Mother writes a letter.

lick

lie

We lie on the sand.

light

The sun gives us light.

like

Does Ben like apples?

like

Alex is like Buster. They are the same.

line

Amy draws a line.

line

We stand in a line.

list

little

Dan has a little apple.

live

We live at home.

long

The balloon is long.

lot

A lot of kittens are in the box. Many kittens are there.

low

The swing is too low.

lunch • lunches

Mm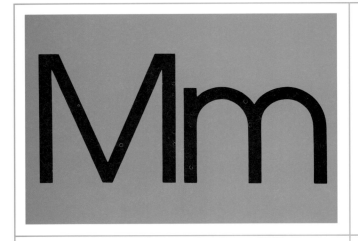

monster

mail

man

men

make   We make a house.

many

Many kittens are a lot of kittens.

map

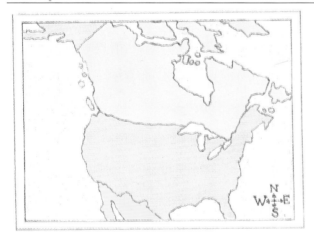

mark

Mother makes a mark.

mark

Ramón gets his mark. It is an **A**.

me

They give me a prize.

meat

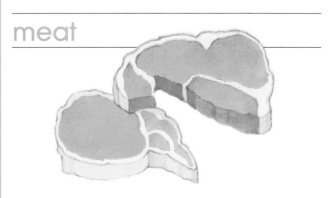

meet

milk

minute

Ching Wah can eat a carrot in a minute.

mom • mommy

Fran calls her mother mom. Dan and Ben call their mother mommy.

money

monster

moon

morning

Morning is the start of the day.

mother

I call my mother mom.

mountain

mouse

mice

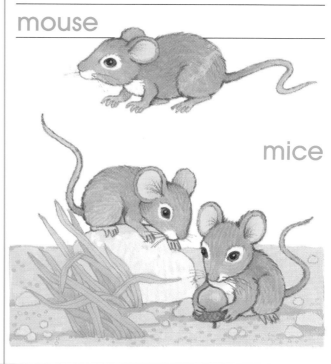

mouth

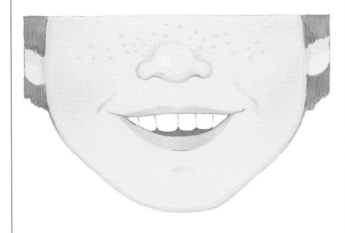

move

The men move things.

music

They make music.

my

Here is my bed.

Nn

nest

name

Ramón   Jill

nap

nest

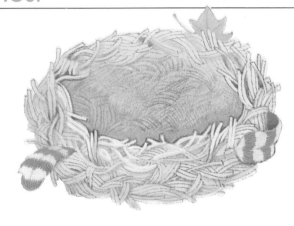

new

The brown shoe is new.
The black shoe is old.

night

Night is the end of the day.

nine

no

Jill says, "No!"

no

She has no bananas today.

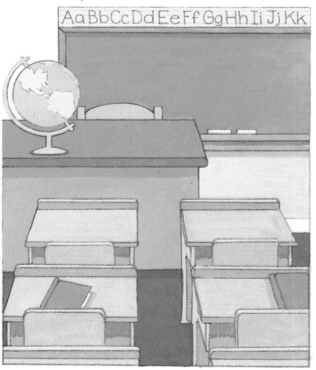

nobody

Nobody is here.

noise

north

The north wind is cold.

not

Freddie does not go.

nothing

Nothing is in the jar.

now

Jump in the pool NOW!

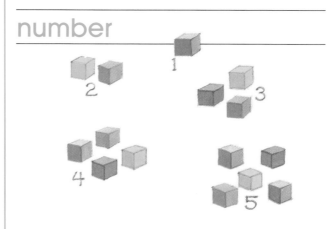

number

octopus

o'clock

It is nine o'clock.

old

The black shoe is old. The brown shoe is new.

one

open

Open the door.

or

Do you like apples or oranges?

orange

It is an orange.

orange

The color is orange.

our

Our dog is Freddie.

owl

Pp

pig

page

The book has pages.

paint

pair

A pair is two of the same thing.

pair of socks

pair of mittens

pair of shoes

paper

park

part   The wheel is a part of the bike.

party • parties

pass

The cars pass the truck.

patrol

pay

peach

peaches

pear

pen

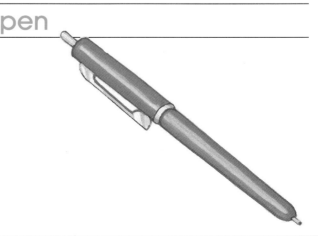

pencil

person

people

pet

The kitten is my pet.

pick

Rob can pick the apple.

picnic   A raccoon goes to the picnic!

picture

pie

piece

pig

pin

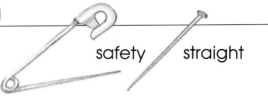

safety   straight

pitcher

May Ling is the pitcher.

place

Jill has a place in line.

plane

plant

It is a plant.

plant

We plant a tree.

play   We give a play.

play

We play with our friends.

please

Please tie my shoes.

point

The pencil has a sharp point.

point

Does May Ling point to the skates?

police

pond

A pond is smaller than a lake.

pony

ponies

pool

potato

potatoes

present

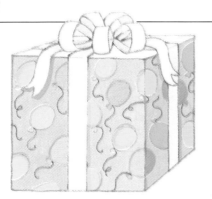

problem

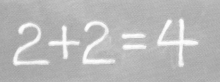

pull

Pull **Freddie.**

prize   Freddie gets the prize.

pumpkin

puppy

puppies

purple

push

Push **Freddie.**

put

Put **the book on the table.**

quarter

queen

question

Jill has a question.

Rr

rabbit

rabbit

A rabbit is a bunny.

raccoon

rain

race

reach

read

Now I read the book.

ready

Ching Wah is ready for school.

red

remember

Did Ben remember his **ABC's?**

rest

We rest after lunch.

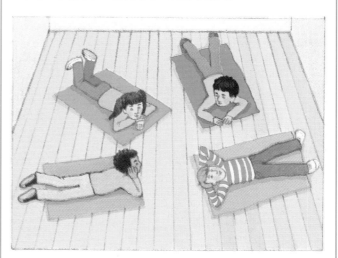

ride

right

Here is Fran's right hand.

right

Annie is right!

ring

Does the telephone ring?

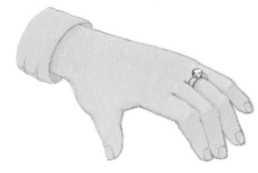

ring

Sara has a ring.

rise

Watch the balloon 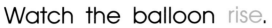 rise.

river

road

robin

robot

rock

rocket

room

Here is Rob's room.

roll

I eat the roll.

rope

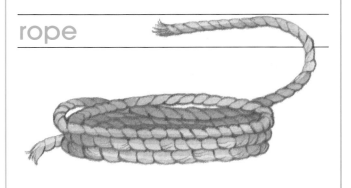

roll   Watch the tire roll.

rose

round

The wheel is round.

row

Row and line are the same.

row

Watch Fran row.

rug

run

Ss

sock

sail

The sail makes the boat go. We sail the boat.

salad

same

Alex and Buster are the same.

sand

sandwich

sandwiches

saw

The saw cuts wood.

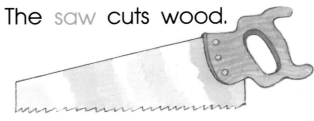

saw

Watch Cassie saw wood.

save

Watch Fran save her money.

say

Say the **ABC's**.

school

sea

seat

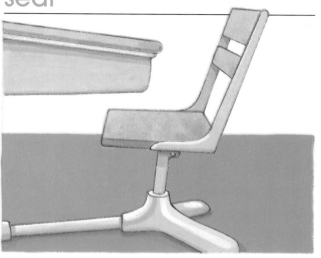

second

Annie is second in line.

see

See the boat!

seed

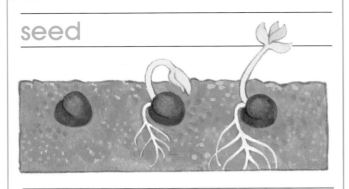

sell

We sell juice.

Orange
Juice
10¢

apple
Juice
10¢

send

We send a present.

POST
OFFICE

sentence

I write a sentence.

set

See the sun set.

set

Otto has a set of tools.

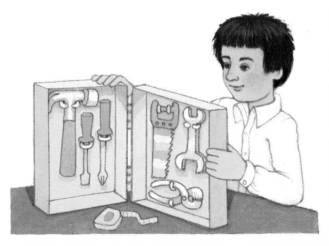

seven

7

sharp

Cassie has a sharp saw.

she

She is Sara.

sheep

Here is one sheep.

sheep

Five sheep are here.

ship

shirt

shoe

shop

Here is a shop.

shop

We shop in the store.

shore

short

Freddie's friend is short.

show

We watch the show.

show

Show me your new watch.

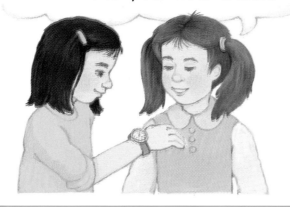

shut

Shut the door.

sick

side

One side of the paper is white. One side is red.

sign

since

May Ling has been waiting since yesterday to swim.

sing

sister

She is my sister. We have the same mother and father.

sit

We sit.

six

skate

María likes to skate.

skate

Here is a skate.

sled

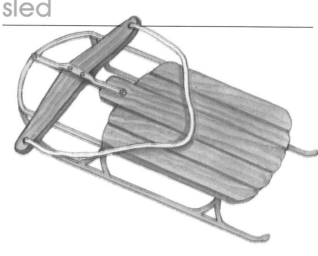

sleep

Ben and Freddie sleep.

sky

slide

small

Dan has the small apple.

smell

The dog can smell a cat.

snow

soap

sock

soft

Too soft!

some

Dan has some balloons.

song

Annie sings the ABC song.

A B C D
E F G
H I J K

sound

soup

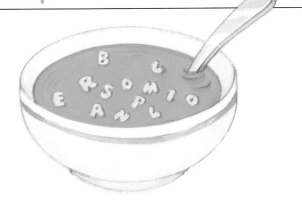

south

The birds fly south.

space

The rockets fly in space.

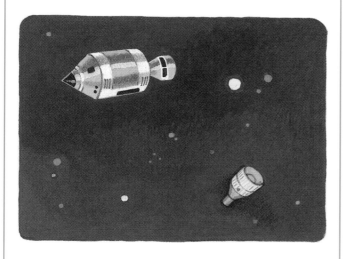

space

Here is the space for a book.

spell

Spell R-o-b.

spring

square

squirrel

stand

star

start

Cassie starts to cut the grass.

station

stay

Freddie has to stay.

step

The first step is red.

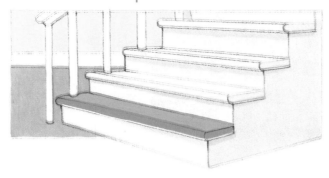

step

The baby takes a step.

stick

Glue makes things stick.

stick

Here is a stick.

stone

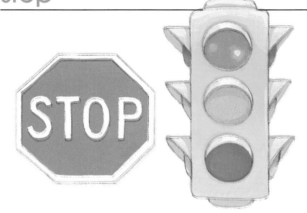

stop

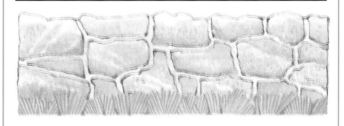

store

storm

story

stories

strong

Dad is strong.

summer

street

sun

supermarket

surprise

What a surprise!

sweater

Her sweater is blue.

swim

Jill can swim.

swing

María is on a swing.

swing

We swing!

T t

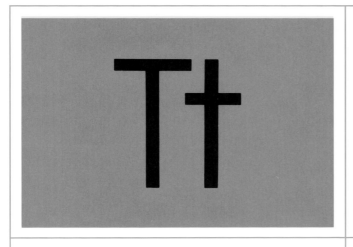

tiger

table

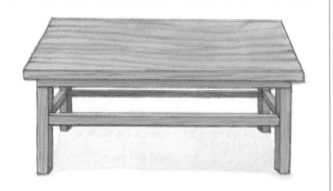

tail

dog tail

kite tail

take

Take **an apple.**

talk

Annie and Fran talk.

tall

He is tall.

teach

teacher

Here is the teacher.

team

telephone

television

tell

Watch Ben tell Rob a story.

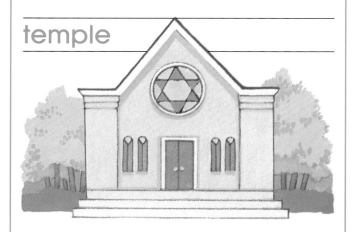

temple

ten

10

thank

Fran can thank Rob and María.

thank you!

Thanksgiving

the

The old brown bear is in my room.

their

Freddie is their dog.

them

Look at them swim!

there

Jill stands there.

they

They hold Freddie.

thing

Here are five things.

third

Ben is third in line.

three

throw

tie

Otto has a red tie.

tie

Mary Jo can tie her shoe.

time

together

We are all together.

tire

tomorrow

today

too

Freddie goes, too.

too

Freddie is too big.

tool

You can make things with a tool.

hammer

saw

drill

toy

teddy bear

blocks

robot

train

The train goes fast.

town

111

tree

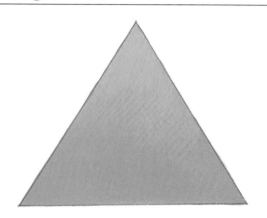

triangle

trip

They go on a trip.

trouble

Max is in trouble.

truck

dump truck

pickup truck

fire truck

try

See Rob try to win.

turn

It is Annie's turn!

turn

Amy can turn the bike.

turtle

two

Uu

umbrella

umbrella

uncle

Uncle Jay is dad's brother.

upstairs

Freddie is upstairs.

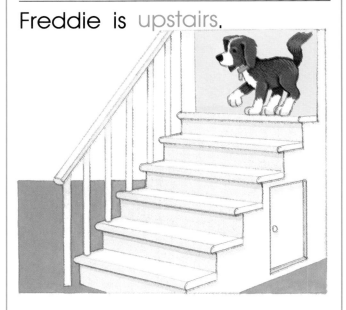

us

Do you have pencils for us?

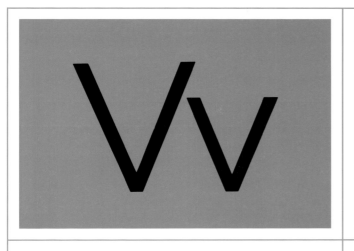

Vv

vest

van

vegetable

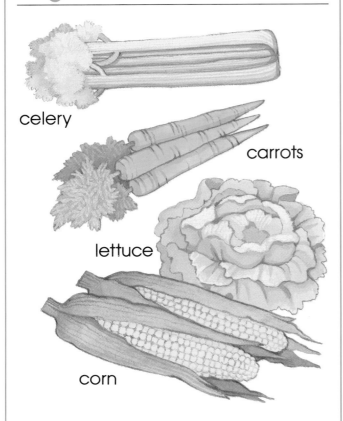

celery

carrots

lettuce

corn

very

Here is a very long dog.

visit

Grandfather and grandmother visit us.

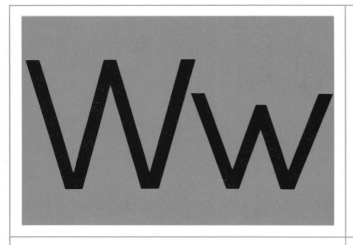

worm

wait

We wait for the bus.

walk

wall

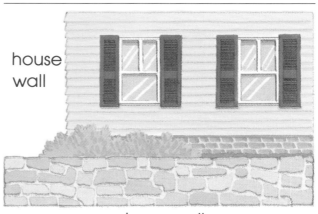

house wall

stone wall

warm

The house is warm. Dan is warm.

was

Ching Wah was the pitcher.

wash

watch
watches

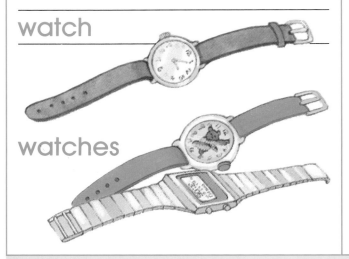

watch

We watch the game.

water

way

They see the way to the zoo.

we

We swing!

week

Seven days make one week.

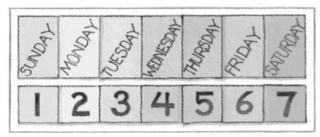

SUNDAY	MONDAY	TUESDAY	WEDNESDAY	THURSDAY	FRIDAY	SATURDAY
1	2	3	4	5	6	7

west

The sun goes down in the west.

wet

what

What does Freddie do? He goes to his dinner.

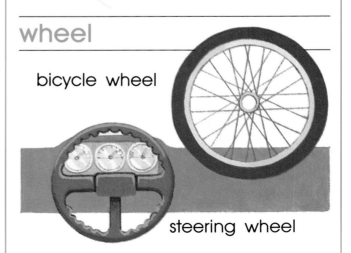

wheel

bicycle wheel

steering wheel

where

Where is Max?

white

why

Why is Freddie wet?

win

Watch Annie win.

who   Who hides from Ching Wah?

wind   The wind blows.

wind

Jill can wind the toy.

winter

window

woman

women

won

Annie won.

wood

word

world

write

Ben can write.

wrong

Sam is wrong!

wrote

Ben wrote his name.

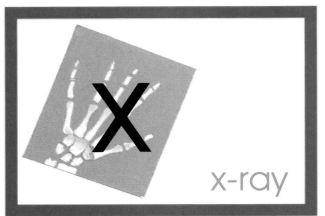

x-ray

x-ray

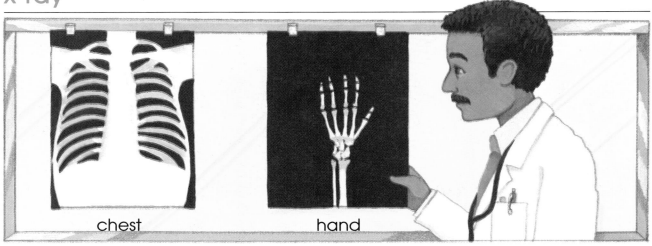

chest   hand

xylophone   The xylophone makes music.

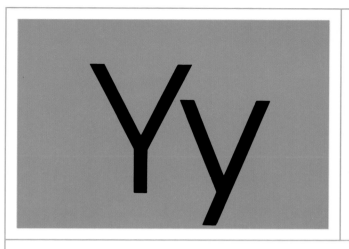
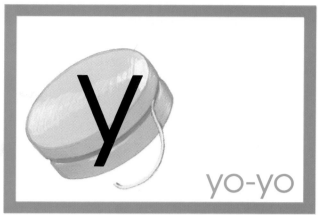

yo-yo

yard

year

May Ling is six years old.

yellow

yes

Yes, she has bananas today.

yesterday

Yesterday was July 7.

you

I am Fran. You are Dan.

young

A young cat is a kitten.

A young dog is a puppy.

A young person is a child.

your

Here is your toy.

Zz

zipper

zebra

zipper

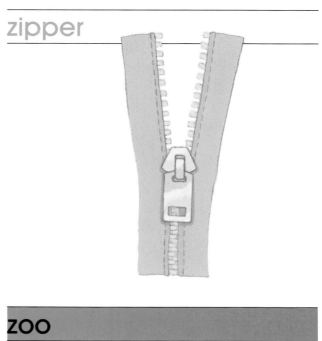

ZOO

zero   Zero is the number for nothing.

Astronaut

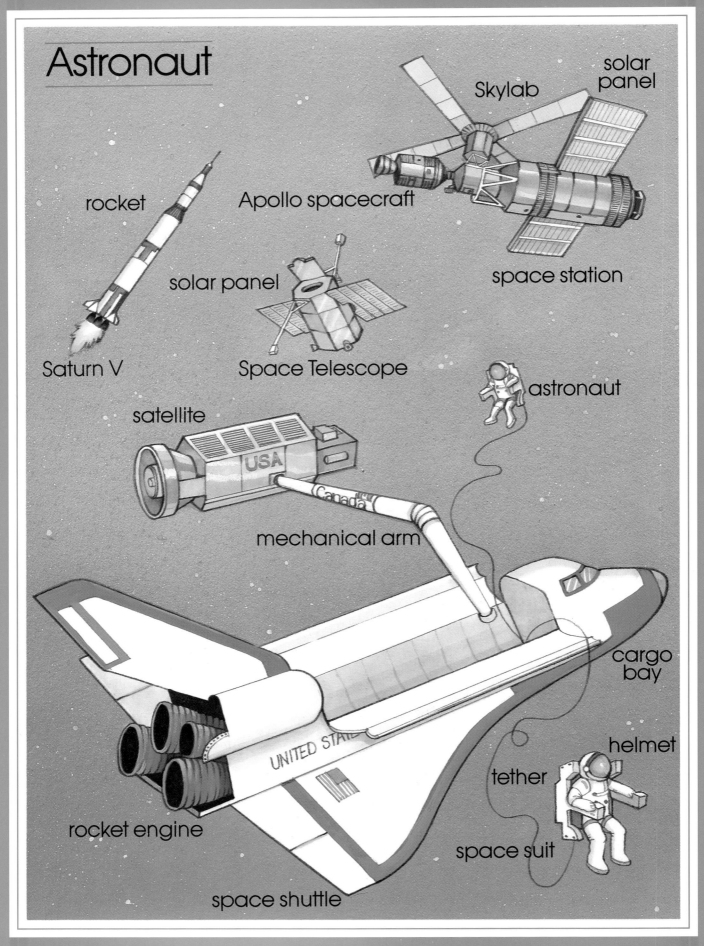

Skylab

solar panel

rocket

Apollo spacecraft

space station

solar panel

Saturn V

Space Telescope

astronaut

satellite

mechanical arm

cargo bay

helmet

tether

rocket engine

space suit

space shuttle

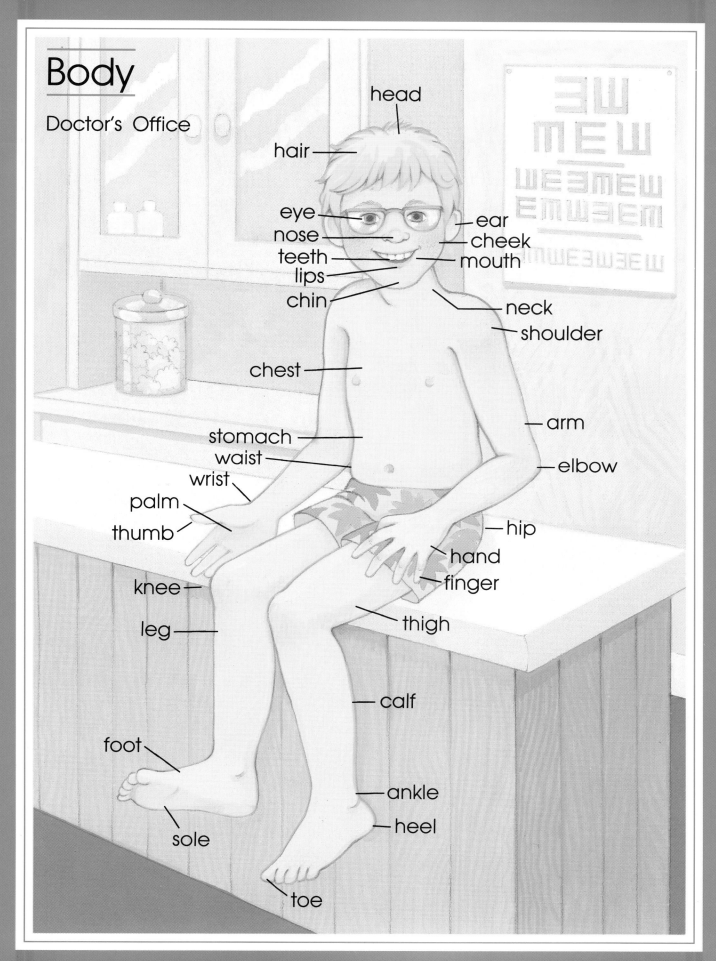

Body

Doctor's Office

head

hair

eye

nose

teeth

lips

chin

ear

cheek

mouth

neck

shoulder

chest

stomach

waist

wrist

palm

thumb

knee

leg

foot

sole

arm

elbow

hip

hand

finger

thigh

calf

ankle

heel

toe

Classroom

bulletin board

aquarium

fish

calendar

handbells

drum

watering can

tape player

drumsticks

piano

songbook

sink

brushes

scissors

construction paper

triangle

toy truck

paint

blocks

easel

toy plane

toy car

window

gerbil cage

plant

chalkboard

1 2 3 4

eraser

chalk

clock

map

globe

teacher

computer

table

Rick

Maggie

chair

sue

aide

cubbies

Reading Group

book

129

Dinosaur

pterosaur

tyrannosaurus

apatosaurus

tricerotops

brachiosaurus

stegosaurus

protoceratops

ornitholestes

Farm

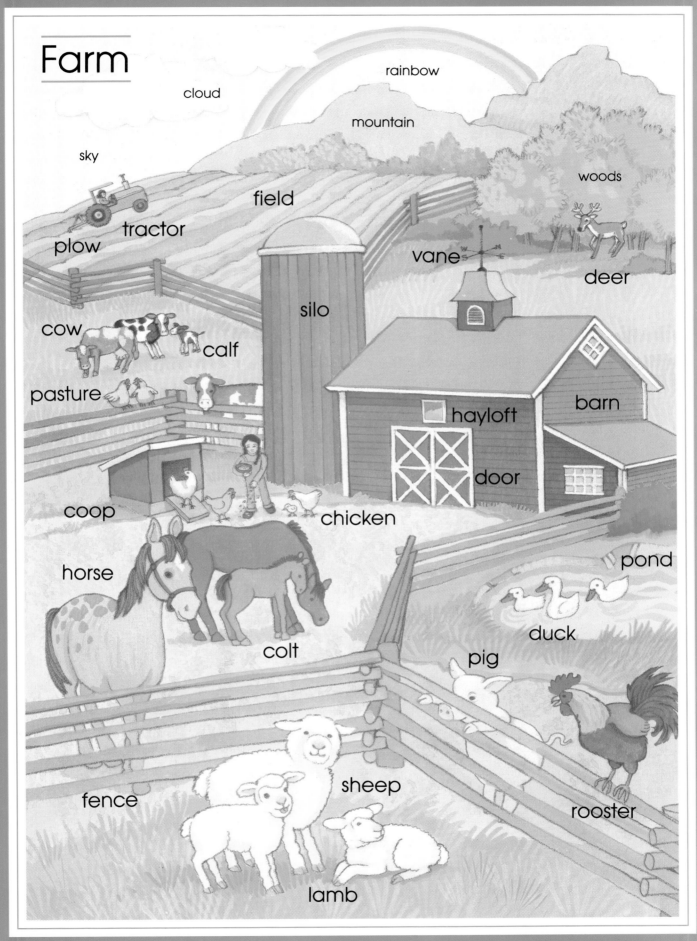

cloud

rainbow

mountain

sky

woods

field

vane

deer

plow

tractor

silo

cow

calf

hayloft

barn

pasture

door

coop

chicken

pond

horse

duck

pig

colt

fence

sheep

rooster

lamb

Games and Fun

bat

baseball

glove

jeans

shorts

hide-and-seek

seesaw

tricycle

hopscotch

sled

toboggan

snow woman

igloo

snowman

kite

wheel

bike

swing

slide

jump rope

pad

shirt

roller skate

hood

snowshoe

ski

snow bird

ear muffs

puck

hockey

mitten

scarf

ice skate

Supermarket

Fruits and Vegetables

tomatoes   lettuce   beans   carrots

scale

fish   chicken   meat

soap

paper towels

corn

dog food

cat food

pears

nuts

potatoes

peaches

cantaloupes

lemons

raisins

peanut butter

basket

shopping cart

limes   grapes

oranges   bananas   apples

door

milk butter cheese eggs yogurt

frozen fish

cereal

crackers

breads

juices

register

counter

cashier

scanner

macaroni

check out

paper bag

bagger

Word

over

under

above

on

across

off

out

in

below

behind

out

Zoo

rhinoceros

zebra

polar bear

elephant

giraffe

hippopotamus

seal

lion

balloon

camel

cub

camera

baby stroller

koala

tiger

walkway

kangaroo